GW00362943

INSTRUCTIONS
FOR
THE BRITISH PEOPLE
DURING
THE EMERGENCY

INSTRUCTIONS

FOR

THE BRITISH PEOPLE

DURING

THE EMERGENCY

Hastily Issued
by the
Department of Unforeseen Circumstances

JASON HAZELEY
&
NICO TATAROWICZ

Quercus

First published in Great Britain in 2020 by

Quercus Editions Ltd
Carmelite House
50 Victoria Embankment
London EC4Y 0DZ

An Hachette UK company

A CIP catalogue record for this book is available
from the British Library

HB ISBN 978 1 52941 194 2
Ebook ISBN 978 1 52941 195 9

10 9 8 7 6 5 4 3 2 1

Typeset by CC Book Production
Printed and bound in Great Britain by Clays Ltd, Elcograf S.p.A.

ABOUT THE AUTHORS

Jason Hazeley

Jason Hazeley is a comedy writer, podcaster and musician who co-authored *The Ladybird Books for Grown-Ups* series and *Cunk on Everything*.

Nico Tatarowicz

Nico Tatarowicz is a comedy writer, actor, podcaster and musician, who has worked on the BAFTA-award-winning *The Armstrong & Miller Show*, *Murder in Successville* and *Crackanory*.

CONTENTS

FOREWORD

As Britain enters a period of tremendous upheaval, your government has requested that everyone immediately undertake a series of life-style changes that may test the nation's resolve.

During The Emergency, it will be for each and every one of us to do their part for the national effort with a strong back, a proud heart and a carefully controlled chin.

This guide, which should be kept with you at all times, and should never be shared with anyone else for reasons of hygiene and paranoia, will instruct you, in plain terms, how you are expected to behave during The Emergency. Most of it is simple common-sense, but common-sense may be new to you, especially if you are young, wistful or an imbecile.

Indeed, it should be noted that much of what is to come in the weeks and months (and months) ahead will be new to us all. But let us remember that, not so long ago, the same was true of pesto.

However, we must not lose heart. With stoicism, courage and a substantial supply of alcoholic fortification, we will pull through this together and emerge from it a stronger (or weaker but more experienced) nation.

Sir Clement Apricot–Wilson
Permanent Secretary
Department of Unforeseen Circumstances

THE BRITISH STORY SO FAR

Britain is* an interesting and varied country. Despite being shy near water, and looking awkward in sandals, it is an island nation that is steeped in history and is furiously proud of itself with little justification.

But Britain is now in a period of tremendous change.

For instance, at the moment, Britain still has a Scotland, but will likely lose it in the coming years when Scotland decides it is big enough to fend for itself and flees for central Europe.

This is likely to make other reluctant Brits, such as the Welsh, the Northerners, the Cornwallingers, the Channel people and viewers in Northern Ireland want to scuttle off as well.

---

* Or, was.

It is possible that, by the year 2040, the United Kingdom will be entirely within the M25, which itself may be largely made from barbed wire and guns.

The 'B-Word'

As you may now have forgotten – through total apathy or sheer panic at recent events – Britain has left the European Union, a 28-nation peace project and trading bloc that most of us had not really thought about until our parents and uncles decided that it must be destroyed. They achieved their aim via something called a 'Brexit' which they had first encountered in the comments section below a video by former disc-jockey and calypso amateur Mike Read.

Some say the Brexit is only a small risk to our wellbeing, along the lines of one of the Beatles recording a solo project, and it being fine, all said, and nobody getting hurt. But that is in all likelihood a false equivalence.

Indeed, Britain branching out on her own may reveal itself to be more akin to someone with a name like Skod-Master-9, who was a minor member of the 400-strong

So Solid Crew, releasing a jazz fusion long-player on Mini-Disc exclusively to subscribers to the *Angling Times*, before humbly having to accept a job at Kwik Fit.

Time will, of course, tell – if there is still such a thing as time after The Emergency. We simply have no way of knowing.

Still, there is little to be gained from being down-mouthed or bloody-throated about 'The B-Word' any longer, not least because nobody will care once their bins are on fire and society has been replaced with There Not Being Anything Any More.

Who Are The British?

The British are a resourceful and imaginative people. They like to imagine they are rather more successful than they are in truth. This is a phenomenon known as 'aspiration' and was introduced after the last Emergency (the Hitler one).

Much of this aspiration takes the form of the acquiring of status, particularly 'orf-the-shelf' middle class-ness. This used to be achieved by well-established networks of respected family names of note breeding and striving for educational excellence, but is now defined largely by television size and a fondness for wasabi peanuts.

In days gone by, the British fell firmly into three camps. They were either chirpily working class, haughtily middle class or horse-botheringly upper middle class (which is what upper-class people call themselves in a rather half-hearted attempt to appear neither hoity nor toity).

Crucially, across the class spectrum everyone agreed that we British had no taste for anything at all, not being French. But then, at some point,* this all changed.

The Invention Of Taste

Somewhere along the way, it became possible to buy art in Homebase, and to listen to the Lighthouse Family on a personal iPod. A third shape of pasta (fashioned to be akin to small helter skelters) arrived in supermarkets. Wine ceased to be used as a cleaning product for front steps or something to be poured on babies' eyes during a churching.

---

* Probably Jamie Oliver.

Where once there were baps, suddenly there were bagels, pitta and focaccia – a kind of Italian sponge that smells of shoes.

Barbour jackets suddenly became popular with the lower orders. The tradition of having a car engine on the front lawn for Dad to marvel at in a cardigan was replaced by paving the garden over and parking a whole car there for each member of the household – even the girls.

The British People discovered and misused new exotic diversions like mange tout (often paired inexplicably with under–developed corn spears), Laura Ashley (and her father and rival Mike Ashley), Zumba, the Greek islands, supermarket sushi, coffee, coffee tables and even coffee table books about coffee (and about coffee tables).

Within the last decade it has become common to encounter a person wearing a North Face coat, who breakfasts not on kippers, but acai smoothies, is heavily tattooed, spends a good deal of time shaping their hair, and has a degree in gin – anywhere from Weybridge to Falkirk.

Oh Dear

Everybody suddenly passing as middle class, whether they were or not, has had a curious effect on the national character.

Being thought fancy seemed to suit everybody initially, because previously the working class was held in disdain by the middle class, and the upper class was held in disdain by the middle class – thus everyone appearing to be middle class put the whole nation on what it thought was an even keel. Sadly too many people were now standing on that keel, and the entire thing sank.

It is interesting to note, at this point in our dwindling global status, that popular and fortunate middle-class people like Lily Allen and the cheese–monger from Blur, who are known to 'cos–play' as members of the working class, somehow still own farms.

Good For A Lark?

The British set great store by their sense of humour. They regard it as among their chief attributes. The ability to laugh in the face of adversity has carried them through many a trouble. It is arguable that they would not have survived such hardships as the horsemeat crisis, Woolworths closing or Sam Smith performing a Bond theme, without the rib-splitting repartee of Ricky Gervais, Prince Philip and Emu.

But their propensity towards seeing the funny side has left the British thinking that anything can be laughed off, and that there is no real danger. The Emergency will, in due course, show that not to be so.

Some things about the British have not changed. They do not like to talk about money, unless it is to complain about somewhere called Rip-Off Britain, which is an imaginary island where everyone is a potential spiv, ready to rinse the unsuspecting Brit of their savings. It does not exist, but is a useful way of characterizing how expensive sausages are on ferries.

But a good deal about the British *has* changed. They are no longer creatures of the stiff upper lip; they do not run on pluck. They are now, instead, a nation of people just sitting there watching screens and *saying things whilst wearing 'jogging bottoms'*.

In times gone by, a family Sunday would find father tinkering with an M.G. in the carport, while mother dug up rhubarb from the garden for that day's crumble. Now, both parents are likely to be watching separate Insta Stories, while the children are watching someone who regards herself as a Social Influencer on TikTok but who may very well be just someone from Tesco who rattles her artificial fingernails on a microphone and calls it A.S.M.R.

But beware – the British mood can turn on a twopenny: people who like to have drunken fights in the street one day will then cry at televised singing auditions the next day.

Change Is Afoot

The Emergency will likely cause very sudden and disproportionate change. For this, we must all be prepared.

There will be disruptions, shortages and surprises. You may find that your energy supply is interrupted, for instance, or that part of your garden is requisitioned by the Ministry of Potatoes.

You may find your milk being delivered by the French Prison Service, or that the only way of obtaining a Nando's PERi–PERi Chicken is with the help of the Armed Forces.

You may find a lack of basic foodstuffs in the shops. But

remember: there is much that can be achieved with prunes and dog biscuits.

If you have not driven your motor-car for some weeks, perhaps get in and remind yourself what everything in front of you is, and what it does, in the event that you are allowed to use the roads again.

There will be new laws to come to terms with, some of which may seem peculiar. Do not be unduly concerned if you or a loved one is arrested for being outdoors.

In your own home, allowances will have to be made. You may have to re-use teabags and tissues. You may have to make your own stock, using water, salt, off-cuts and pets. You may have to eat anything you find under the shed; or the shed itself.

You will be spending many hours at home, so be thrifty and imaginative. Make the most of self-isolation.

What Is Self-isolation?

Self-isolation is the noble act of removing yourself physically from the local community and staying in your own home, because the government has deemed it vital to your safety. When such measures are in place, they must be observed strictly until The Emergency is over. Low intelligence, male privilege or a cavalier attitude does not preclude you from doing your bit.

Some people, like the elderly, divorced cat–owners, professional drummers and oddballs have been self–isolating for many years and may barely notice any difference when such rules are enforced.

The rest of us may find it a tad intense – and, in short order, one could find oneself experiencing a combination of dread, delirium and an increased fascination with one's own pleasure apparatus.

You will not need much to get by during The Emergency, but it is wise to invest in a moderate (but not socially irresponsible) supply of tinned pilchards, kitchen roll and a good pair of thick curtains.

If you are self–isolating with children, there is a good chance they will see the opportunity to destroy you psychologically and replace you in the pecking order. Guard against this by knowing where there is a spare supply of Celebrations, which can be used as either persuaders or bribes.

Gin and loud music can nullify the feelings of parental

exhaustion to a point, but ultimately it is *you* that must bring your children under control whilst still appearing to love them.

Some Things Not To Do
While Self–isolating

Lighting an indoor bonfire

Drying your clothes in the oven

Trying to drink gas

Burrowing into your neighbours' garden

Commenting on a Russell Brand video

Decorating using mayonnaise

Trying to combine multiple children into one

Going upside down (it won't make any difference in
the long run)

Boiling your legs

Swapping underwear, however tempting it becomes

Looking 'in' your television

Opening your mail

The Stereophonics

PARENTING DURING
THE EMERGENCY

Home Schooling

Children will need your firm hand in guiding their education. Likely, their schools will have prepared work schedules for them. Do not be alarmed if some of the subjects mean absolutely nothing to you. S.T.E.M. and S.P.A.G. are not fanciful notions your child has just dreamed up – they are part of the curriculum, as you would have known had you taken even the slightest interest in their education until now.

Certain areas, like maths, English and 'topic', suit home schooling better than others. Among those not to attempt are:–

Swimming

Metalwork

Choir

Foreign exchange trips

Fire drill

Nativity play

Fencing

Abseiling

Chemistry (especially magnesium)

Bear in mind that you may be visited by a representative from Ofsted (in a chemical suit) who will want to thoroughly inspect your premises and regime. Make sure you have a safeguarding policy, an up–to–date D.B.S. check, robust risk assessments and a complete set of lesson plans ready, or you may be shot on sight.

Entertaining The Little Ones

Many traditional simple childhood games lend themselves very well to a societal lock–down scenario. You might be of a mind to try some of the following:–

Teddy Bears' Picnics

It remains safe for soft toys to congregate in large numbers if they are sterile. However, it is advisable to keep them in a bin–bag in the garage at night and to put them through a laundry cycle after their time outdoors. During The Emergency, it is advisable not to give teddy bears or your children the impression that eating generous quantities of food outdoors remains morally defensible. Instead, try a different tack – say, Teddy Bears' Diets or Teddy Bears' Detox. What could be more fun than young Ted going keto for a spell?

Kite Flying

While it may appear safe to go out and fly a kite in an empty field, one has to bear in mind that the conditions for being able to do so will allow any airborne diseases you are carrying to be transmitted up to a thousand miles from your mouth or nose. For this reason, it is recommended to make a simple paper kite that is fastened to a rod of bamboo and simply look at it. Or, better still, put your superstition to one side and let your child hold an umbrella in a sealed room.

Tiggy-Through-The-Window

Similar to traditional 'Tig' (also known variously as 'Tag', 'Tic-Tac-Toe' and 'Catch the Twat'), but in which the host player remains in their own home while a young friend circumnavigates the building trying to catch sight of them through the glass. Ladders can be used to check upstairs bedrooms but all windows must remain locked. Try to discourage squealing as it tends to draw hen-pecked middle-aged men into their gardens to demand some quiet.

Knock Down Ginger

Touching other people's doors is not advised at this time. A better way to enjoy a game of Knock Down Ginger is to send someone a blank email. Of course, they will know it's from you, but this is a time of sacrifice, and each of us must play his part.

Red Indians

Running around a wig-wam in the garden dressed as a cartoon Indigenous American and going 'woo woo' is safe, but the child should not repeatedly dab their mouth with the palm of their hands, which will ideally be strapped to their sides.

Kebab Shop

Children love playing shop. And, in the midst of The Emergency, it gives them a gentle introduction to a now much bleaker world. (You might also see it as an opportunity to teach them the value of money and the reality of a compromised food supply chain.) In the game Kebab Shop, potato peel, envelopes or even shredded utility bills can be used to represent 'chips in pitta' and bowls of iceberg lettuce. Tired shoe insoles or dry cat food make fun replacements for high-street night meats and falafel. This game is best played in the early evening before the adults are too drunk.

Fun With Fluff

There is much that can be done with a humble quantity
of fluff. It can be used to make a pretend moustache.
It can be rolled into a very tiny ball. It can be put on
a hamster's head to make it look like Mrs Slocombe.

Children And Swearing

Children should be permitted to use coarse language
throughout the duration of The Emergency. Swearing is
an excellent stress reliever, is good for morale and gives
the little ones a sense of control over events they are likely
to be confused about.

It is sensible, though, to implement a few simple rules.

The F-word should be avoided at the dinner table
unless somebody bangs their shin or burns themselves
on a dish.

The C-word should be considered a week-end treat
unless you are discussing politicians, reality television stars
or people ignoring serious medical advice.

Racist language should be avoided completely unless

your child is particularly adept at impersonating their own grandparents or other bigoted adults that are known to them. In this case it may be considered a liberal form of irony, within reason.

STAYING HEALTHY
DURING THE EMERGENCY

Personal Hygiene

You may find yourself at the mercy of a local or national toilet paper shortage. Do not worry unduly if this is so, because there are a great many substitutes you may deploy, such as:–

Leaflets from local pizza parlours
Socks (but not your own)
Bread which is past its best
Photographs of your significant other's former partners
Any correspondence suggesting you owe money
Supermarket recipe cards you picked up years ago
    and used once
Enticing propaganda from local estate agents
Anything from Pound World

Big mice (allowing for mutations)
Receipts (since all guarantees no longer exist)
Sushi

Household Cleanliness

You may also encounter a shortage of cleaning products.
And, once you have exhausted the vinegar and the entire
home smells like chip-papers, you will have to find other
ways of doing the weekly wipe-down. The following can
be re-purposed as cleaning products:–

Your trouser pockets
Lager
Tea towels
The dog
Wet grass
Snot
'Geoff'
Anusol
Milk
Fire

Enjoying Sports In Confined Spaces

Some sports can be adapted to be played in smaller than usual venues. For instance:-

Cushion rugby (not for Grandma)

Miniature surfing by standing on a tray in the bath

Bench pressing the children

Human dressage (or Crufts)

Hands-free badminton by blowing a feather to and fro

Shadow judo (not recommended on cloudy days)

Table tennis using two flip-flops and a sprout

Extreme forward rolls in moderation

Dry kayaking by sitting pillion in a child's cot and using air oars

Hoover tossing having unplugged the machine first

Vegetable snooker with each other's mouths as pockets

Synchronized sitting (do try not to cheat)

Pole-vaulting into the neighbour's garden using the washing-line prop

Stair luge (speaks for itself)

Cock fighting (for groups of male students)

Cupboard wrestling (as played at Eton)

Ignoring Conspiracy Theories

There will be an oversupply of opinion during The Emergency, much of which will be nonsense.

People will say it is a man-made event designed to cause colossal economic hardship. They will say that everyone is exaggerating it (which itself is an exaggeration). They will say it will go away when the wind changes or the clocks go forward. They will say it was predicted in the Bible or *The Simpsons*. They will say it is the fault of the Italians, or the vegetarians, or the sweaty.

None of this is true. It is rich piffle. But there will be a small but vocal horde of clever–dicks (and dickesses) who would rather believe that there is a dark, twisted truth to be revealed, often inexplicably linked to Zionism. These people are themselves simple and twisted, and should be ignored, ridiculed or sedated with pellets.

Likely Reactions And Your Mood

You may find that your emotions are heightened during The Emergency, leading you to partake in behaviours that you would usually think the better of.

The truth of the matter is that people cope with a change in the fabric of civilization in different ways. One of the most popular ways to deal with a situation one is unused to is by *not coping at all.* This technique can feel natural and comforting at first, but after a few days, you may find it leads to high blood pressure, soiled clothing and suicidal pets.

Your teeth may yellow, and substances that are usually reserved for a celebration might begin to look like breakfast. Check this list of behaviours and try to ascertain which category you are currently falling into.

If you find yourself in Category C, do us *all* a favour and stop it at once.

Behaviour Check-list

Category A (Expected)

Scurrying about

Frowning

Regularly burning toast

Using coarse language whilst looking for keys

Grimacing at news reports over the sound of a child's
    requests

Assuming the worst whilst wearing a dressing-gown
    all day

Bleaching unusual surfaces

Attempting to use music recording equipment

Eating butter on its own

Holding one's breath in Morrisons

Intending to start yoga

Category B (Cause For Concern)

Skulking about, hiding under cars etc

Rictus smiling

Hoarding toast in one's cheeks

Ransacking one's own house to locate keys

Allowing children to create their own laws

Assuming the worst, having put the dressing-gown
in the outside bin

Bleaching your hair and hands whilst singing nursery
rhymes

Sharing your latest heartfelt ballad with disinterested
acquaintances

Wearing butter

Entering Morrisons wielding a cricket bat

Internalizing one's yogic failings

Category C (Cease Immediately)

Jumping from rooftop to rooftop

Smearing excreta on your face

Building a shelter out of toast 'bricks'

Burning down your house, whilst your family look
on aghast

Training your children in lethal arts

Turning your new inner reality into a pamphlet (dressing-gown recovered but soiled)

Drinking bleach whilst screaming/laughing

Inviting beleaguered friends to watch you perform music on a live stream

Buttering your entire house

Entering Morrisons in a car which has been armoured with kitchen implements

Doing yoga

Pulling Yourself Together!

If you are behaving as per the examples below, it is time to give yourself a thorough talking to. A bathroom mirror will suffice. However, if your mirror is now drawing solar energy on the roof of your dwelling, you can shout at your reflection in a stainless steel kettle or serving spoon.

Screaming is appropriate at a Beatles concert in 1963, or if a madman is loose with a high velocity rifle. It is NOT appropriate in the crisps aisle at Morrisons.

Panic buying may seem shrewd when a state of war has been announced. In fact it is a sign that you are vulnerable to becoming a conduit for evil.

Asking the postman to leave your package in the park is a bit much. The poor blighter has been up since four. In addition, your parcel is likely to get eaten by foxes. Or children.

Contacting former lovers. He, she or they moved on from you a very long time ago. Allow them the dignity of trying to process the end of the world without your reminding them of how jolly a time you had in Rhyl two decades ago.

Crying again. You were understandably crying earlier today, but now you are doing it again, even though you have watched your favourite three films back-to-back. Stop it.

TAKING YOUR MIND
OFF THE EMERGENCY

Fun Things To Do At Home

Turn a shoe into a dog by putting googly eyes on it, attaching it to a piece of string and taking it for a 'walk'.

Make your own jigsaws by dropping crockery.

Name all of the radiators in your house and ask your family to test you on them.

Invent a language made of humming where you have to do that rubbing–your–finger–up–and–down–quickly–across–your–lips thing to swear.

Make up a window–cleaning dance by soaping your casements with your shampoo–covered buttockry.

Colour in the bricks on your walls with chalk or Sharpies. If you look online, you may find some interesting patterns, or ways to spell out messages of hope or hopelessness or draw Space Invaders.

Establish a league table of human-spotting with a simple scoring system – say, 1 point for a human going past, 10 points for a member of the emergency services and 100 points for archbishops.

Write a novel but not in the expectation that it will be published, just to see if you 'have a novel in you'. If it transpires that you do not 'have a novel in you', see if you 'have a shelf in you' or 'have a salad in you'.

Make your own bidet by standing on a box backed up to your designated sink holding a spoon behind you to divert the flow of water from the tap upwards, to its desired destination.

Mindfulness And Relaxation

It has become fashionable in recent times to imagine that one can simply focus on the present in order to dispel one's woes and make oneself 'at one' with the vibrations of the outer universe. Whilst this may work well during an economic boom, you may find the technique rather blunted by the very real possibility that everything you have worked for is now worthless and there is nothing left to eat but salt and socks.

This is not to say that intense focus, in and of itself, is not an effective relaxation tool; just that it might be wiser to channel your efforts into concentrating on something that also has a practical use and may aid the survival of your immediate family. Creating a secure nuclear bunker in your spare room, or stripping your car of parts and re-purposing them as home-made weapons can be both satisfying and sensible.

Remembering The Before Times

Here are some things you might like to reminisce about:-

Shops
Soap
Brexit *Question Time* special
Jobs

Weather
Influencers
Shapes
Vans carrying panes of glass
Brian May
Frittatas
Match of the Day
Cowboy boots
Paddy McGuinness
FitFlops
Lions
Buskers
David Cameron humming
White pepper
Cardboard masks of Camilla Parker Bowles
Liverpool
Murals
Drum (and bass)
Mars bar milk–shakes
Walking along
Teeth
Cars
Robert Dyas

Josh Widdicombe's voice

When your clothes used to fit

Electricity

Yams

Your PIN number

Hugging friends

Anything else

Coping With Pod-cast Anxiety

Many people like to use pod-casts to distract themselves from their inner turmoil and forthcoming nervous collapse. But **be warned**. There are now over forty million highly recommended pod-casts to choose from – and every man jack of us now has a great many friends recommending we listen to a great many conflicting shows on the same subject: sport, for instance (which no longer exists) or current affairs (which no longer exist).

Pod-cast indecision can lead to a feeling of overwhelming helplessness. And yearning for a time when Adrian Chiles was still popular.

If you find yourself growing impatient when choosing

a pod-cast it is probably wise to just keep listening to the introductory sections of The Adam Buxton Pod-cast until the point at which his dog Rosie runs past.

If you are without a viable pod-cast listening device and are in need of emotional relief, talking to yourself in a child's voice and rocking backwards and forwards is still a very passable substitute.

Recipes For The Emergency

Cooking is not traditionally part of the national arsenal, but these are unique times. Ready meals may be in short supply; in which case, you will need to prepare meals from scratch. Even then, ingredients may be in short supply; in which case, you will have to use your imagination. Here are some simple ideas.

Space houmous. If you leave the Arabic pea-sauce known commonly as 'houmous' to one side for long enough, it will begin to fizz. This is excellent alongside high meat or bread that can nearly walk.

Potato crumble. Make some crumble topping out of the bits accumulating on your fireside rug and throw it over a load of mash in some dish or other. An affordable 'treat' that also makes a passable mince if one is drunk.

Shower mushrooms. A variety of mushrooms can be grown indoors by simply not opening the bathroom window for a few weeks. And in the absence of herbs, any leftover colognes or perfumes make a good herb 'lacquer' for a dash of French.

Potatoes on toast. Speaks for itself. Works with all types of potato except baked, in which case the toast should be folded in half and inserted into the cleft of the potato.

Surprise water. Water, but with an unexpected ingredient – like a cigarette or a coin. Another element of the surprise is how filling water can be. For example, one can easily fill a bath or even a pond with it!

Pulled bread with sweet potato photographs. A touch of the good old days with a fashionable twist. Vegans should avoid pictures of animals or milks.

Rice cakes. For when there really is no such thing as food.

Communicating With Friends And Family

During The Emergency, you can still stay in touch with those you love over video messaging services like Face-Time, Skype or the watches from *Doctor Who*.

Remember, while general conversation and sociable to-and-fro is easily achieved, some things are rather more difficult in this virtual realm, and it is not advisable to try any of the following activities in this way:–

Tennis
Dentistry
Deep tissue massage
Boxing
Voodoo
Pet grooming
Group sex
Microsoft Excel

Betting As A Family

Assigning a parent as the household's bookmaker is an excellent way to raise the stakes and inject fun into even the most mundane domestic situation. Mum or Dad shouting the odds on what time the cat will come in, or when the dog might lick his or her own underneath tends to foster a healthy sense of camaraderie that soon becomes infectious, and even addictive!

Children as young as four can be encouraged to become familiar with the intoxicating thrill of gambling, and it also helps to sharpen their arithmetic.

However, it is important to keep it fun, and not allow any family members to fall too deeply *into the red* as financial injustice is a fast–track to violent disagreements.

It may be wise to keep one eye out for unscrupulous older siblings quietly buying debts from a drunk or tired parent after a hard day, trying to run both a house and a school from the same dining table.

Selling As A Family

PRACTICAL ADVICE
DURING THE EMERGENCY

You can find a generous amount of advice in a series of government leaflets which you may collect from your local post office, field hospital or council checkpoint. These include:–

Hiding an elderly relative
Dealing with the local bell-end
Securing a roundabout
Hot–wiring an ice cream van
Blackmailing your employer
Suburban hunting and the law
Navigating an armed jumble sale
How to make wearable disease filters
Stealing your own identity
Self–defence, your rights and murder – a fine line?

How to think like an Ewok

Simple grenade ideas for the kids

How to get protein without touching anything

Using National Trust property as a garrison

Bribing private doctors

Family militia group dynamics

Home-made psychotropic drugs

Prison – the better option?

Starting your own religion

Using water tokens

PERSUADING YOUR FAMILY
TO HEED ADVICE

Managing Your Children

There comes a time in a person's life* when it becomes apparent that they are the only person in their family capable of rational thought.

On a car trip to the Welsh sea-side, this needn't cause any bigger problem than ignoring a whining voice whilst you try to find a notoriously quiet A-road. During The Emergency, however, it may feel as though you have been promoted to Commander-in-Chief of a jar of flies.

Children come with their own problems, but you are bigger than them, and you can devastate their supply of digital pursuits. Now is the time to revel in their

---

* At the age of 43.

technological addiction, and use it to implement the government's advice to your own ends. They will have to get over it.

Managing Your Elders

Your own parents and any older relatives in your orbit might not be so easily manipulated – often seeming to actively *want* to seek out the ascribed danger like a racist lemming heading towards a cliff.

Their daily ideas about how they aim to go about their business during The Emergency are likely to be comically unwise and wildly dangerous. But beware – exasperated laughter at their absurd notions will only drive them to insist upon them more.

Wanting to go and have a look at the danger, making sandwiches for the insurgents and posting unsound medical advice on their Facebook pages are all things to keep an eye out for from Mum and Dad.

But don't be too hard on them. After a certain point,*

---

* At the age of 59.

parents pass a cut–off that does not allow them to acknowl-edge any sense of wrong–headed–ness at all. Especially if it is being highlighted by someone to whose very rectum they can remember applying Sudocrem.

The easiest course of action, unless you want to shout and cry yourself hoarse, is to let go of them emotionally altogether. One technique is to phone them to say you love them, but without allowing the conversation to go any fur-ther. Upon placing the receiver down, wish them good–bye out loud, whilst staring into the middle distance, and then turn your attention to something more fun.

If you live under the same roof and your parents make your *own* home a place of conflict and tension, you may be able to come to an arrangement with a local farm in a fruit–picking capacity until things return to normal.

MONETARY ADVICE
FOR THE EMERGENCY

The nature of money will change during The Emergency.

With so few places to spend it, you would think that the typical citizen would find themselves well provided for. But this is not so.

With their labours suspended, most people will find themselves short of a penny. After all, they must still eat – and most gardens from The Before Times contain not a replete vegetable patch, but a trampoline, which is far harder to peel and boil.

If you are low on funds, you may be able to come to an understanding with the owner of the local corner shop or the C.E.O. of Asda.

If you are in tremendous debt, you may find yourself

– refreshingly – surrounded by admin you are no longer scared of. After all, this is a fine time to ask your creditors precisely what they plan to do about recovering money from anyone, when no–one has any.

Conversely, if you are fortunate enough to be wealthy, this is an excellent moment to treat yourself to a little something, like a favourite pub, village or yacht.

In the event of the complete collapse of the monetary system, a new currency based on pasta will be introduced. The values will be as follows:–

Penne = 1 penny
Fusilli = 5 pence
Farfalle = 10 pence
Rigatoni = 20 pence
Conchiglie = 20 pence
Ravioli = 50 pence
Tortelloni = 1 pound
Lasagne = 5 pounds
Spaghetti Bolognese = 10 pounds
Tuna pasta bake = 20 pounds

Tagliatelle with Taleggio and freshly shaved black
truffle = 50 pounds*

Avoiding payment will become a common-place. There
will be those, for instance, who will join up the characters
on their motor-vehicle's number-plates, the better to fool
any recognition systems in filling station cameras. This is
not advised, even though it works.

There are other ways of avoiding payment, such as:-

Putting spelling mistakes in your address for your
energy provider

Pretending you're deaf

Not answering the phone unless it says MUM

Posing as your own housekeeper

Staging your own funeral

Disguising yourself as a shopping trolley

Re-training as a gangster

Meditation

Taking refuge in a church

Registering as a charity

---

* Includes complimentary glass of Chianti.

A military coup
Joking one's way out of it
Using the phrase, 'You cannot prove I'm not a food
   bank'
Putting a kidney on Ebay and saying it's signed by
   Sting

WORKING FROM HOME
DURING THE EMERGENCY

A good many people will find they are able, with the help of available apps, to work from home. Using Zoom or Houseparty, groups of people can communicate with each other online in real time. So it will still be possible to hold all those unnecessary meetings that are so vital to modern business.

Not everyone can work from home. But you can at least operate on the pretence that you are.

For instance:–

If you are a plumber, check all your own taps and make some small, unnecessary but chargeable alterations here and there.

If you are a dentist, have a family member lie across

your lap while you hold their mouth open with chop-sticks and shine a head torch down their throat with a look of intense professional curiosity.

If you are a nail technician, attend to your toes, pretending they are the hands of a large, unwieldy customer who is not among your regulars.

And if you are a bus driver, arrange all the chairs in your house into four rows and sit ahead of them ignoring anybody running alongside you.

But you may find that all your professional skills are surplus to requirements now. In which case, The Emergency may be an excellent opportunity to re-train as, say, a virologist or a disaster capitalist.

The Emergency may also be a good time to start an insurance company, provided you insure it against failure or future Emergencies.

DEALING WITH YOUR 'URGES' DURING THE EMERGENCY

Going It Alone

There are a great many ways of enjoying solitary carnal pursuits. Most obviously, ones involving specialist pleasure equipment bought from the splendid collections of Ann Summers, Lovehoney and companies of their ilk. But if you lack these bedroom basics, there are a great many ways to improvise, such as:–

Pushing oneself against a vibrating item like a tooth-brush or vacuum cleaner;

Disrupting the blood flow to one hand before any manual undertaking, so it resembles the cold touch of a fascinating stranger;

For the gentleman, taking unusual advantage of a bath sponge, covered in cling film and rolled into a tight enclosure;

For the lady, sacrificing a well–oiled cucumber to the nether cause. (Avoid pickles.)

Zero–Contact Pleasure

For a non–messy alternative to the above, it is useful to try to concentrate VERY hard on a formative moment in your reproductive development. For example, the first time you became aware of the taut physique of a screen idol or came across the shower section of the Argos catalogue, or caught a glimpse of Jennifer's bosom or Colin's ridge. Perhaps you can recall a foray into manual stimulation behind the bins of your local cinema. That's it. Now – breathe. Good.

Continue these thoughts until you feel a pulsing behind your knees. You have now reached 'drygasm'. Congratulate yourself and move on. That is *quite enough* of that.

Common or Garden Intercourse

What happens between two (or more) legally bound adult humans is nobody's business but theirs and, in some cases, their local council's. (Check your sports centre notice-board for particulars and bye-laws.)

In any case, 'it' should remain a private and serious matter.

One partner may prefer to get in the mood by reading in bed patiently, keeping noise to a minimum, whilst the other attends to their teeth and gums. Beyond that, we offer no guidance. You are on your own. Just don't do anything likely to cause a fire or dislocated joints. And avoid hot wax.

Ideally, couples should assign the cellar (or shed, if you have one) for conjugal activity and private rummaging. Try to keep it down a bit, but, if you MUST make a noise, bite down on the handle of a hammer or a pet's sterilized chew-toy.

Perverts

Just because we are making a combined effort as a proud nation, it does not follow that your local spittle–monkey, helmet–flasher or throb–prowler has changed his ways. With street–lighting dimmed to save us all money, it will be harder than ever to spot Dirty–Desmonds, cat–shouters and over–mothered fun–boys nestling in the shrubs. Be vigilant.

Remember – make a sketch of any perverts that decide to take up residence in your garden IMMEDIATELY. Do not leave it until the next day. You can be sure that you will approximate your memory of the offender with your own prejudices and unwittingly draw someone along the lines of either Jeremy Corbyn or Ross from *Friends*.

These sketches can later be submitted to a jury, and compared with the court artists' sketches of known wally–wangers for verification when the legal system is up and running again. This is a rough but effective system that saves valuable time with trials. And, besides, it is generally accepted that most perverts are guilty.

IF YOU MUST GO OUTSIDE
DURING THE EMERGENCY

Football Hooligans

Naughty faces and top boys from rival firms must meet on abandoned land, such as that around disused factories, and may only arrange one-on-one meetings or 'offs'.

Be sure to stand at least six feet apart. Throwing projectiles at each other is permitted, provided disposable gloves are worn. Anyone running away before making a good fist of avoiding injury with their guile may be considered a 'melt' (unless the Old Bill show up) and may be subsequently roundly mocked under a YouTube video of the event.

Boy Racers

Car races on abandoned roads are permitted between two vehicles. However, inviting an attractive lady wearing tight jeans to start the race by standing between the participants' cars and dropping a handkerchief is dangerous and unnecessary. Three co-ordinated toots of the horn should suffice.

Cricket

Cricket is permitted, but must be played without a ball, wearing dark colours. This is what the forces called 'Sly Man's Cricket'. No field is too big for a game of Sly Man's Cricket during The Emergency, and it can be played by boys, girls and well-trained dogs.

In fact, spreading out so far as to have to telephone each other instructions on the theoretical whereabouts of the 'ball' is advisable – as is not joining in at all to keep the game 'low-key'. Use your discretion.

Hide Not Seek

This adaptation of a childhood classic game speaks for itself. Hiding is permitted; seeking is not.

Remember, we all must preserve our energy in case we should be required to run for our lives towards a fleet of crammed buses before they leave for the Channel Tunnel. That said, it is imperative to keep your spirits up. So take turns nestling yourselves away in a loft, under some tarpaulin in a car-port, or – if you live in a block of flats – in the least urinated upon area of the bin store.

The game itself is easy enough, but it *is* important to agree on some sort of time-scale when playing as, in some cases, unclear rules have resulted in disappearances, starvation and children having their eyes pecked out until they are skeletons.

If your child has been hiding for longer than 90 minutes, it may be time to shout their name. Children under five can usually be located very easily by their feet, which are sticking out of the curtains, but from six upwards a child with moderate skill can very easily spark a local manhunt. Should this happen more than once, ignore it.

WHAT TO EXPECT
AFTER THE EMERGENCY

Human Behaviour

For all of us, it will have been a long time since we have interacted with each other in a way that we would previously have characterized as normal and found as easy as falling off a cliff.

Therefore, it follows that we may find ourselves a little rusty on the basics. There will be behaviours and protocols we have forgotten.

For instance, many people will have forgotten the basics of personal hygiene. It may not be the case that everyone smells very agreeable. Some may smell like a French kidnap or a sauna full of turnips. Make allowances for this.

Similarly, do not hair-shame anyone; it is beastly. We

will all have spent a great many weeks without the help of a hair professional, and everyone will look shaggier, greyer and more unkempt. Or, if they have attempted to cut their own hair, they may resemble someone from a 1970s Freemans catalogue.

It will also have been quite some time since people engaged in even the slightest physical contact – let alone anything as familiar as a hand–shake or a hug. Do not be alarmed if someone punches you in the nose because you brush past them in a shop or if someone screams their eyes out when you go in for a polite kiss. These will be trying times, and we must make allowances for those unfortunate souls who will have lost all that remained of their minds during The Emergency.

Do not become frightened of pubs. They may begin to loom over you on your solitary night–walk, whispering their stories of a forgotten world as you pass. You might feel the need to shudder, or worry that you have forgotten how to interact with your fellow man. But HEED THIS: pubs and clubs are going to need you to *up your intake* when The Emergency has passed. Therefore it is a good idea to drink more than you usually would on a nightly basis in your home, unless you are due to go into labour, are under 13 or are overly religious, in which case check with your local parson or mufti.

Your Work–life

Remember that you have a job, if you still have a job, and that your job has a work–place, if it still has a work–place. Look up where it is and re–familiarize yourself with the route you take to get there. It may be advisable for you to perform a rehearsal run before your first day back.

And remember to dress appropriately for your job. If you work in an office, wear sensible office–wear. If you are a mechanic, wear overalls. If you are a chef, wear whites. Do not wear pyjamas, whatever your job. You may have become accustomed to wearing pyjamas *all the time*, but certain social protocols are sacrosanct, and nobody wears pyjamas to work.*

When you are back in the work–place, remember that your job probably does *not* require you to spend six hours arguing about the relative merits of the contestants on

---

* Except the actor in the 'secret lemonade drinker' advertisement.

Celebrity MasterChef on social media. This is not vital to the national economy, and is just a bad habit you have fallen into whilst stuck at home, like nose–picking or meth.

Wildlife

While we humans are away from the streets, it is possible the foxes may take over. The fox is, as we know, a wily and greedy beast, and will almost certainly seize upon this opportunity to consolidate its burgeoning power base.

At minimum, the foxes will attempt a military coup, which will likely have been masterminded by the owls.

Dogs will be fatter now. Cats may have vanished, most likely by befriending sailors, hiding on ships and moving abroad. Or they may be inside the dogs.

The Changing Nature Of Importance

There will be things of great importance that you will have forgotten, abandoned or neglected. These can include:–

Your health
Your waistline
Your public hair
Your private hair
Your VAT returns
Your colleagues' names
Your friendships
Your storage unit
Your teeth
Your library books
Your Pilates classes
Your children
Your mortgage
Your ambitions

You must try to remember what things were important in The Before Times, because they may well return to importance when The Emergency is over.

But for this we must wait and see, because it may be that the importance or triviality of things has changed wildly during The Emergency.

Be prepared to adjust to a very different set of priorities.

We may find that the most surprising things are suddenly important – perhaps spinach, reggae or handstands. And that previously very important things, like your spouse or your job, are now irrelevant.

DOS AND DON'TS

Don't start a comedy vlog unless it can be empirically shown that you have a sense of humour.

Don't worry about the country running out of money, because by the end of The Emergency, the C.E.O. of Zoom will be the richest man in the world and able to bail us all out.

Don't cancel your wedding: instead, say it is hazmat–themed.

Do spread your Christmas out to stretch the entire year. Do the turkey the minute you see a turkey. Do presents when you've had long enough to make presents. Leave stockings until autumn, when there might be fruit.

Don't start a riot in Waitrose by shouting, 'They're out of Seedlip!'

Don't answer the door to anybody unless you are prepared to kill them.

Do keep any musical instruments handy – they may be pressed into service as weapons. The same is true of the family tortoise.

Don't buy crisps off Amazon; they have enough to do.

Do try to re-use ice cubes, glacé cherries and cocktail sticks.

Don't pay for anything with banknotes; they may be needed as food.

Do be wary of friendliness; it is likely to be a ruse intended to result in your death.

Don't become inwardly sour. Do it outwardly.

Do keep your mind sharp by performing little mental exercises, like calculating your phone number in base seven or writing out the lyrics of 'Hotel California' backwards.

Don't have any more children. They will be a burden.

Do try to get used to the taste of surplus Campari.

Don't kill insects. They may become our main source of protein.

Do try to put Crufts out of your mind. It is not going to happen for a very long time.

Don't go on a booze-run to France. You will be even less welcome there than usual.

Do learn a new skill such as impersonating football managers and dead celebrities.

Don't smash your windows from the outside. Always from the inside only.

Don't expect too much from your cat. The poor fellow may have no real grasp of what is happening.

Don't buy Frosties – Corn Flakes are perfectly adequate.

Do make your own 'throwing stars'.

Don't forget to fill in your cloning form. This is a legal requirement.

Don't sell your children's teeth. You will deflate the price of teeth by over-supply.

Don't *go on* as if *you* invented flat-breads.

Do make your box-sets last. There will be no more for many years.

Don't be so bloody rude.

Don't panic. Everything will turn out just fine.

Do bear in mind that the above may not be true.